Our Holi

The Hindu Festival of Colours

It is Holi.

Holi is a time we say thank you.

This is a **bonfire**.

We will make a bonfire at Holi.

5

We will sing

and we will dance

at Holi.

Look at the **paint**.

The paint is red and blue and pink.

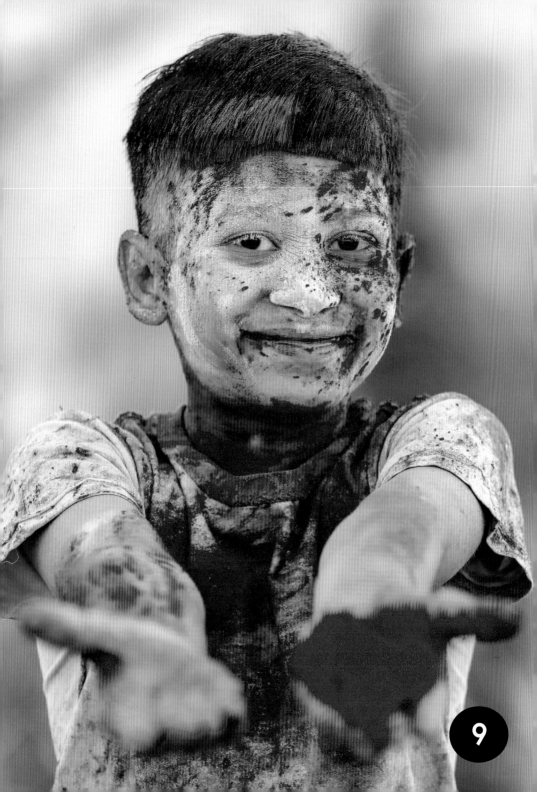

We will have fun throwing the paint at Holi.

11

Look at the food.

The food is good to eat.

13

Look at my friends.

I am having fun

with my friends

at Holi.

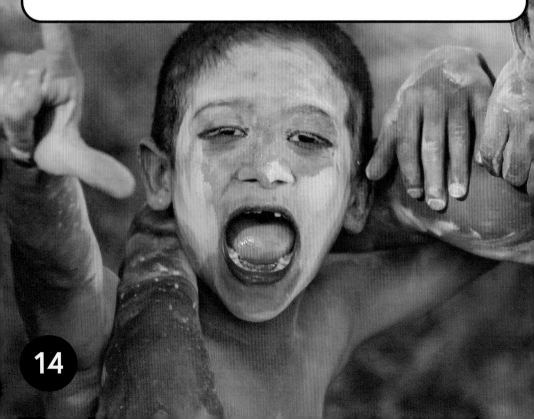

15

Glossary

bonfire

paint